MW00411970

CONTENTS

Chicken Noodles – Tina Klaus
Pork in Marsala & Red Wine – Dana Bisenius
Teryaki Pork – Pheobe Labine
Sweet Potato Bisque – Julia Norman
Granny's Macaroni Cheese – Shani Raviv

Sweets & Puddings

'Eaton Mess' – Francesca Baker
Flourless Pomegranate and Coconut Brownies - Tori Hauschka
Heavenly Almond Bread – Nikki du Bose
Superfood Truffles – Christine Bailey
Rum Balls – Nina Mills
Blueberry Oat Cake – Chris Sandel
Brown Sugar Swirl Cake with Buttercream Icing - Jessie Moore
Queen of Puddings – Thereza Baker
Fruit Cocktails – Jamie Malcolm

Nitty Gritty

Thank you
Contact details

INTRODUCTION

We need food to live. All the actions, thoughts and thrills that come with a full and thriving life require energy from a balanced diet to fuel them. But sometimes a little help is necessary.

There are many misconceptions around eating disorders, but one thing that is clear is that the relationship between a person and their food can improve and even become healed. Learning to love and connect with one's self and one's food again is a huge step on the path to recovery and a healthy relationship with food, and thus being able to nourish the body to live the life it is made for.

Of course food is not just about nutrition. Meals can be a very enjoyable experience, a social galvaniser and a pleasurable way to mark points in the day. This is a book of recipes to educate and support, and help food become an enjoyable experience which nourishes body and mind.

Submitted by people with an experience of eating disorders, either personally suffering, recovered, carers or other people involved, the collection here is a gathering of recipes that have stories attached to them. There's meals that evoke memories of childhood, those tried for the first time in recovery, those lost in the ill years and found again, and more.

Some of the recipes may seem terrifying, and others a little more familiar. Try them and challenge yourself, not letting yourself be limited by rules. Be compassionate with yourself, taking care of yourself as you step a little way outside of your comfort zone. Everything in here can be part of a balanced and healthy diet, and has been checked by nutritionists in accordance with NHS guidelines. So use the opportunity to experience new tastes and new experiences as you journey through whatever recovery means to you.

Eating disorders are complicated, and not all about the food. But food is a crucial part of recovery. Embracing its role as medicine, fuel, social connection and enjoyment is all part of the process. This book is designed to help you and, by the profits going to BEAT UK, other individuals, to do just that.

I hope you find the book helpful, the stories powerful, and the meals delicious, and the process healing.

Francesca

How To Use This Book

This book is not meant to replace dietetic input and advice from you nutritionist. Please discuss with the appropriate expert your own personal needs.

Each recipe is marked with the food groups that it covers, if served in the correct portion, at a meal. Portion sizes are based on the guidance given for a healthy adult, and outlined on pages XXXX. Get guidance from a dietician if you want personal advice, but remember that this is eventually what you are working towards.

Calories are not included, as the book is designed to help you move away from counting and rigidity - but it does complement a routine, as a gentle reminder that a balanced diet needs to contain carbohydrate, protein, vegetables/fruit and fats.

You can replace certain ingredients:, for example chicken with turkey, or alter the level of spices. If you don't like something, perhaps try it again, tweaking an ingredient or two. If you struggle don't give up. If it doesn't look quite right, who cares? It's all a learning process. Enjoy it.

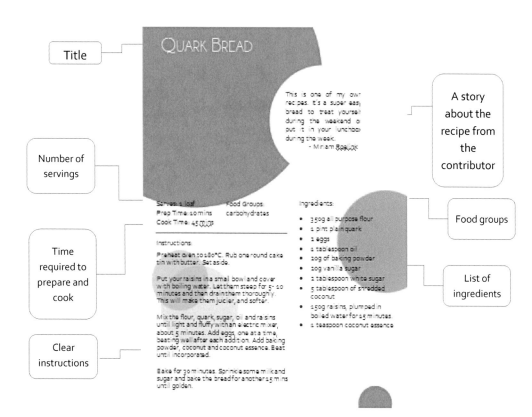

A BALANCED DIET

A balanced diet contains all of the food groups - starches and carbohydrates, protein, dairy, fruit and vegetables, and fats. Each meal should contain elements of each, and a good guide to portioning is to use the rule of thirds. On a standard size dinner plate one third should be carbohydrate, one third protein, and one third vegetable, with 1 - 2 tablespoons of oil/fats used as dressing or spread. Throughout the day try to have the following number of servings.

The Eat Well plate has been developed to give guidance for a balanced and healthy diet. It's important to remember however that during recovery your body is repairing damage caused by malnutrition, and therefore your need for certain food groups may be greater.

Food Group	Servings per day
Starches/Carbohydrates	6 - 8
Protein	2 - 3
Dairy	2 - 3
Fruit & Vegetables	5 - 7
Fats/Oils	3

It's one thing eating the right foods, and another making sure that you get enough of them. These are examples of the different food groups, and approximate serving sizes. Remember too make sure that you are getting enough, but also not to get too caught up in exact measurements - some apples will be bigger than others, sometimes you will have more milk on your cereal. It's ok! As long as you can honestly say that you are getting enough food to fuel your body, don't worry about a gram or two.

STARCHES/CARBOHYDRATES

Starches provide a slow and steady release of energy throughout the day. These starches, or carbohydrates are sugars that break down inside the body to create glucose. Glucose is moved around the body in the blood and is the primary source of energy for the brain, muscles, and other essential cells.

Cereals, grains, pasta, breads, crackers, snacks, starchy vegetables, and cooked beans, peas and lentils are all good examples.

2 slice bread
1 bagel
1 English muffin
1 medium roll
40-70g cereal
50g rice
50g cous cous
75g rice
50g bulghar wheat
300-500g baked potato
4 small/medium new potatoes
6 cups popcorn

PROTEIN

Protein is essential for the healthy growth of all of your body tissues – such as your muscles (including your heart), internal organs (such as your lungs and liver) and skin – and also for repair of these tissues.

A wide variety of foods contain protein, including meat, fish, dairy, eggs, nuts and pulses.

150gm cottage cheese
50 gm cheese
200g pulses/baked beans
2 eggs
30-40g nuts
120g chicken breast
120g tin tuna/salmon/sardines
120g fillet fish
120g pork/beef

Fats

The fats you eat give your body energy that it needs to work properly, keep your skin and hair healthy, and insulates your body to help keep you warm. As well as this essential fatty acids are needed for brain development, controlling inflammation, and blood clotting.

1/2 medium avocado
30-40g nuts
30-40g cheese
1 teaspoon margarine/butter 1 teaspoon
1 tablespoon mayonnaise
2 tablespoon sour cream

Fruit & vegetables

Fruits and vegetables contain a variety of nutrients including vitamins, minerals and antioxidants, essential for healthy functioning of the body. They are also an important source of fibre.

80 g vegetables
1 fresh fruit
200gcanned fruit
250ml fruit juice
40g dried fruit

Dairy

Dairy products are a good source of energy and protein, and contain a wide range of vitamins and minerals. They are rich in calcium, necessary to build healthy bones and teeth.

Think cheese, yoghurt, milk, oily fish and dark leafy greens.

125 - 180g flavoured yoghurt
200g - 250g plain yoghurt
250ml whole milk
30-50g cheese

Sugars and sweets

Sugars are a type of carbohydrate and are easily broken down by the body, becoming an immediate form of energy. Plus they taste good, and sometimes that is reason enough!

Cakes, biscuits, yoghurts and sweets are all tasty choices.

5xm wide slice cake
1 doughnut/muffin
45 - 50g chocolate bar
2 - 3 biscuits
2 - 3 scoops ice cream
125 - 180g flavoured yoghurt
200g - 250g plain yoghurt
1 granola/snack bar
200g custard/rice pudding

MEAL PLANNING

To help you plan your meals for the week and ensure that you have adequate nutrition and enjoyment out of your diet, here's a meal planner - and some handy tips.

Remember the rule of thirds - roughly a third of your plate should be carbohydrate, a third protein and a third vegetables, with dairy and fats included in this.

Don't be too rigid - if something tastes good, is nourishing you in some way, and you know that it's a 'normal' meal or snack, eat it. Try to get some variety in, for both your physical and mental wellbeing.

When unsure about your choices, ask yourself whether you would encourage a younger sibling or someone you care very much about it to eat it. If it's good enough for them it's good enough for you.

Meal	Mon	Tues	Wed	Thurs	Fri	Sat	Sun
Breakfast							
Snack							
Lunch							
Snack							
Dinner							
Snack							

SHOPPING

Food shopping can be hard and supermarkets a difficult place to go when suffering from an eating disorder or during the process of recovery. Here are some tips to help you overcome those challenges.

- - - - - - - - -

Keep a pad and pen in the kitchen - when you've got through the last of your favourites scribble it down on the list. Take the list! If you see something else you like the look of note it down to try next time.

Shopping for specific ingredients with meals in mind and taking a list helps ensure we use what we buy, and lessens the chances of feeling confused or overwhelmed. Thinking about ingredients that can be used in multiple dishes, planning both quick meals and those involving more cooking, with your schedule in mind, will all help.

Check use by dates and ensure that fresh food will last long enough.

Build in enough flexibility to your plan. If the first choice product isn't there, what can you pick that is 'good enough?'

Try to go shopping with a friend or family member if possible to help reassure, support and validate your choices.

Don't go shopping hungry - it adds a whole other dimension to what is already a difficult time.

If you find yourself compulsively checking nutritional information, try basing your decision on different factors e.g. price or flavour. Give yourself a time limit to choose, then move on to the next item on your list. Give yourself a criteria, and pick on that. For example, if you are choosing a ready meal, decide that you want one including chicken, that takes less than 15 minutes, and take the first one that fills that criteria.

When choosing loose fruit and vegetables, try closing your eyes and picking up the first one your hand comes to. Don't worry about how you look – most people are far more focused on themselves!

Visiting a smaller supermarket with a smaller range can be less overwhelming, as some of the element of choice is reduced.

Think about what will support you. If planning ahead works, go shopping once a week, with top ups for fresh goods. If having too much food in the house is a trigger, go more often.

If it all gets too much, go to a non food aisle for a few minutes, and take some time to breathe.

Always have the essentials for a basic meal in your cupboard, in case you feel you can't face shopping today, or something comes up.

CARBOHYDRATES

PROTEIN

FATS

FRUIT & VEGETABLES

DAIRY

SNACKS & SWEETS

CONDIMENTS

BREAKFASTS

QUARK BREAD

This is one of my own recipes. It's a super easy bread to treat yourself during the weekend or put it in your lunchbox during the week.

— Miriam Roelink

Serves: 1 loaf
Prep Time: 10 mins
Cook Time: 45 mins

Food Groups:
carbohydrates

Ingredients:

- 350g all purpose flour
- 1 pint plain quark
- 2 eggs
- 1 tablespoon oil
- 20g of baking powder
- 20g vanilla sugar
- 2 tablespoon white sugar
- 5 tablespoon of shredded coconut
- 150g raisins, plumped in boiled water for 15 minutes.
- 1 teaspoon coconut essence

Instructions:

Preheat oven to 180°C. Rub one round cake tin with butter. Set aside.

Put your raisins in a small bowl and cover with boiling water. Let them steep for 5 - 10 minutes and then drain them thoroughly. This will make them juicier, and softer.

Mix the flour, quark, sugar, oil and raisins until light and fluffy with an electric mixer, about 5 minutes. Add eggs, one at a time, beating well after each addition. Add baking powder, coconut and coconut essence. Beat until incorporated.

Bake for 30 minutes. Sprinkle some milk and sugar and bake the bread for another 15 mins until golden.

SIERRA LEONE RICE BREAD

At one hospital I received treatment at there was a nurse that used to smile all the time. He also used to bring in this rice bread all the time. I think his wife baked it and it reminded him of her and home. He smiled whilst he ate it anyway!
- Francesca Baker

Serves: 1 loaf
Prep Time: 40 mins
Cook Time: 60 mins

Food Groups:
carbohydrates

Ingredients:

- 350g all purpose flour
- 3 bananas (over - ripe)
- 200g rice flour
- 100g sugar
- 100ml groundnut oil
- 1/4 teaspoon grated nutmeg
- 1/4 teaspoon salt
- 75ml water

Instructions:

Heat oven to a medium temperature and grease loaf tins.

Mash bananas in a mixture bowl into a smooth pulp.

Stir in sugar and flour alternately, beating well after each addition. Add small amounts of water until a dropping consistency is reached.

Add salt, nutmeg and oil. Stir well and allow the mixture to stand for about half an hour to soften the starch granules.

Pour mixture into greased loaf tins and bake in a moderate oven for about 1 hour. Test it is cooked by pushing a skewer into the centre, which should come out clean.

Cool and serve in slices.

BLACKENED EGGS WITH AVOCADO

This light brunch or supper is full of protein rich eggs and cheese plus avocado adds vitamins C and K and folate. Eggs also contain selenium and Vitamin B12 with plenty of calcium in the cottage cheese. The blackened eggs have a lovely Japanese flavour so if you like sushi rolls, you'll love this dish.

- Laurel Alper

Serves: 2
Prep Time: 2 mins
Cook Time: 5 mins

Food Groups:
carbohydrates, protein, vegetables, dairy

Ingredients:

- 4 large eggs
- 300g pot cottage cheese with onion and chives
- 2 tablespoon soy sauce
- 6 shitake mushrooms
- 4 slices of bread
- Half avocado

Instructions:

Beat the eggs well.

Add cheese and soy sauce and whisk into eggs, then add mushrooms covering with egg mixture.

Pop the mixture into microwave for 2 minutes then remove and give mixture a good whisk, then put back into microwave and cook for further 2½ minutes. Cooked to perfection, the eggs are full and fluffy.

Serve with avocado on toast.

PORRIDGE

I forgot how much I loved banana porridge. An eating disorder is not worth missing this for.

- Jess Wells

Serves: 2
Prep Time: 2 mins
Cook Time: 5 mins

Food Groups:
carbohydrates, protein, vegetables, dairy

Ingredients:

- 50g porridge oats
- 300ml milk
- 1 banana
- 1 tablespoon honey

Instructions:

Place the porridge oats into a saucepan and add the milk. If you have time you can soak them overnight, but if not, place onto stove on medium heat.

Heat for 5 - 10 minutes until thickened, stirring occasionally. When cooked, take off heat.

Mash the banana and serve on top, drizzle with honey, and enjoy.

Superfood Smoothie

An easy way to fuel your body first thing, or as a snack - with no cooking required!
- Bek Young

Serves: 1
Prep Time: 5 mins
Cook Time: 5 mins

Food Groups:
carbohydrates, protein, vegetables, dairy

Ingredients:

- half a ripe avocado
- 1 tablespoon of flax seeds
- 1 tablespoon of goji berries
- 1 handful of washed and roughly chopped curly kale
- 1 date
- 125g of frozen raspberries
- tablespoon pomegranate seeds
- 250ml milk

Instructions:

Combine all ingredients in a blender and blend until smooth and creamy!

LUNCH TIME

Quadruple S Salad

Lately I've been trying all sorts of things to see how it makes me feel and how much energy it gives me. The best part of this salad is that you can really tailor it and make it your own. Think of this as your base and dress it up however you're feeling.

- Katie Dalebout

Serves: 1
Prep Time: 5 mins

Food Groups:
fats, protein, vegetables

Instructions:

Mix all the ingredients up in a big bowl and use your hands to massage it together so it all incorporates well.

Serve with a carbohydrate of your choice - pitta bread works well.

Ingredients:

- 4 cups finely chopped argula
- 2 - 3 tablespoons apple cider vinegar
- Squeeze or two of fresh lemon
- half of a large avocado (or a full small one)
- alfalfa sprouts or broccoli sprouts (any kind of mild sprouts)
- pinch of sea salt
- 1 teaspoon cinnamon
- ½ teaspoon cardamom
- dash of cayenne
- shredded coconut
- optional sweet breakfast toppings include hemps seeds, blanched almonds. goji berries, cacoa nibs, sliced banana, granola, nuts, pumpkin seeds, sunflower seeds

PITTA POCKETS

My philosophy is based on good eating well rounded meals. as often as possible. Casual and easy, this is a great meal for those nights when your family are coming and going. Quick to throw together and portable, so it can be eaten on the run. Or place on a large plate in the middle of the table and let everyone make their own.

- Jodie Blight

Serves: 4
Prep Time: 10 mins
Cook Time: 3 mins

Food Groups:
carbohydrates, protein, vegetables

Instructions:

Preheat oven to 160°C. Wrap the pita bread in foil and warm for 3 minutes in oven.

To make yoghurt dressing, mix all sauce Ingredients: in a bowl. Taste and adjust to your liking.

Remove pitta from the oven and lay the ingredients down the middle of the pitta bread. Spoon over dressing, wrap and devour!

Ingredients:

Meal

- 50 g vermicelli rice noodles
- 2 tablespoon coconut oil
- 4 wholemeal pita bread
- 400g cooked lamb, warm
- 1/2 red onion, finely sliced
- 250 g cherry tomatoes, halved
- 1 Lebanese cucumber, sliced
- 2 handfuls baby spinach leaves

Yoghurt dressing

- 4 heaped tablespoon Greek yoghurt
- 2 tablespoon mint sauce
- 1 garlic clove, crushed
- 1 handful mint leaves, chopped

Miso Ramen

I made a variation of these every day for dinner the first week I moved home after a hospital admission It was my way of taking care of myself in defiance of no one else knowing how to take care of me, and simple enough to make that it didn't require a lot of energy.

- J Jhor

Serves: 2
Prep Time: 5 mins
Cook Time: 15 mins

Food Groups:
protein,
carbohydrates,
vegetables

Ingredients:

- 2 tablespoon instant miso paste
- 300g soft tofu
- 2 cups leafy vegetables (e.g. Chinese broccoli, spinach, cauliflower, brussel sprouts)
- 200g noodles
- 1 tablespoon Korean red pepper paste
- 1 tablespoon chopped ginger
- lemon juice
- soy sauce

Instructions:

Dissolve miso paste in 500 ml boiling water in a small pot.

Add flavorings to taste and simmer for 10 minutes.

Chop up the vegetables and tofu (into medium sized cubes).

Add the vegetables to the pot, followed by the tofu.

Cook over medium heat for 5 minutes,

Serve immediately with noodles.

CHEESE ON TOAST

Serves: 2
Prep Time: 1 mins
Cook Time: 2 mins

Food Groups:
protein,
carbohydrates,
dairy, fats

Ingredients:

- 2 slices of white bread
- 2 teaspoons butter
- 50 - 60g mature cheddar cheese

Instructions:

Butter the bread, then place it butter - side up in the grill.

Toast it until the butter side is crispy and golden. Next, remover the half toasted bread (careful not to burn fingers) and place the cheese on the non toasted, non buttered side. Replace under the grill, cheese - side up this time and leave until cheese is browned and bubbly.

Remove from the grill and eat.

(Buttering and grilling the underside of the bread first gives it an extra buttery crunch that is sensational!)

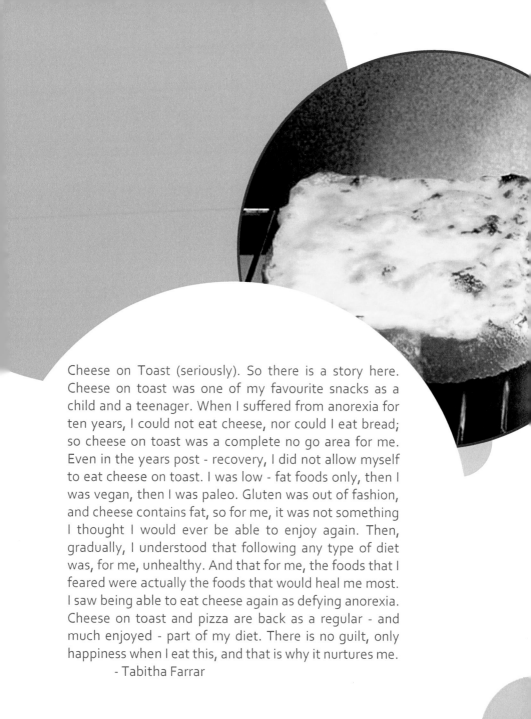

Cheese on Toast (seriously). So there is a story here. Cheese on toast was one of my favourite snacks as a child and a teenager. When I suffered from anorexia for ten years, I could not eat cheese, nor could I eat bread; so cheese on toast was a complete no go area for me. Even in the years post - recovery, I did not allow myself to eat cheese on toast. I was low - fat foods only, then I was vegan, then I was paleo. Gluten was out of fashion, and cheese contains fat, so for me, it was not something I thought I would ever be able to enjoy again. Then, gradually, I understood that following any type of diet was, for me, unhealthy. And that for me, the foods that I feared were actually the foods that would heal me most. I saw being able to eat cheese again as defying anorexia. Cheese on toast and pizza are back as a regular - and much enjoyed - part of my diet. There is no guilt, only happiness when I eat this, and that is why it nurtures me.

- Tabitha Farrar

Hobz Biz-Zejt

This reminds me of family holidays in Malta when I was young. On a Sunday we would go to the beach, my mum, dad, brothers and sisters and cousins. At lunch time numerous Tupperware boxes would be removed from cool boxes. The Maltese bread would be sliced fresh and these were made for us all. Once the basic bit was done each of us could choose what we wanted on top. It still is the first thing I order on my holidays.

- Rebecca Pierson

Serves: 1
Prep Time: 10 mins

Food Groups:
protein, egvetables, fats

Ingredients:

- 1/2 onion chopped
- 2 slices crusty bread
- 20ml olive oil
- tomato paste or sliced fresh beef tomato
- 120g tin tuna
- 4 - 6 anchovies
- sliced onion
- capers

Instruction

Put a dessert spoon (10ml) of olive oil on a plate, enough to cover the boase.

Take one thick slice of crusty bread. Place one side down in olive oil and let it soak up for a few seconds .

Next rub over top of the same side with tomato paste or half a fresh tomato.

Add toppings and salt and pepper to taste.

French Pistou Tomato Soup

This tomato soup recipe is inspired by a French cooking lesson I had in Stanmore. The highlight of this soup is definitely the amazing Pistou sauce that's served on top!
- Tu Dinh Tran

Serves: 4 - 6
Prep Time: 45 mins
Cook Time: 60 mins + 4 hours

Food Groups: carbohydrates, protein, vegetables

Instructions:

Place the beans in a saucepan, cover with boiling water and simmer for 20 minutes.

Drain the beans and cut them in half, cut the leek into fine slices, and carrot/turnip/zucchini into small dices.

Heat the olive oil in a large saucepan and sweat the leeks for a few minutes. Then add veg, sweat for another few minutes, before adding the white beans and stock, diced tomatoes and tomato paste.

Season with salt, pepper, thyme and bay leaf. Bring soup to the boil, and reduce to simmer, for a further 20 minutes.

Add green beans and pasta. Continue cooking for another 5 - 10 minutes until all vegetables and pasta are tender.

To make the Pistou sauce, puree basil leaves, chopped garlic, olive oil & cheese in a food processor. until mixture is smooth.

Ingredients:

- 400g can of cooked white beans
- 1 tablespoon olive oil
- 100 g leek
- 1 carrot
- 50g turnip
- 50g green beans
- 1 small courgette
- 400 g canned diced tomatoes
- 2 tablespoon tomato paste
- 50g macaroni pasta
- 1 litre of chicken or vegetable stock
- 1 pinch of dried thyme
- 1 bay leaf
- Salt & pepper to taste

Pistou Sauce

- Small bunch of basil
- 1 clove of garlic
- 2 tablespoon of grated cheese
- 2 - 3 tablespoon of olive oil

Creamy Broccoli & Cashew Nut Soup

Serves: 4
Prep Time: 20 mins
Cook Time: 10 mins

Food Groups:
vegetables, fats

Instructions:

Place the stock, garlic, ginger, cashews, fish sauce, vinegar, tamari in a large saucepan and bring to the boil.

Add the broccoli and simmer for 5minutes until the broccoli is just tender.

Process the soup in a blender to create a thick, smooth soup. Add the oil and process again to combine. Season to taste.

Spoon into bowls and drizzle with a little tamari to taste.

Serve with bread for your carbohydrate portion.

Ingredients:

- 2 tablespoon olive oil
- 1 litre vegetable stock
- 2 cloves of garlic, crushed
- 1teaspoon ginger finely grated
- 80g cashews
- 1teaspoon fish sauce
- 1 tablespoon apple cider vinegar
- 1 tablespoon tamari
- Sea salt and black pepper to taste
- 500g fresh broccoli, cut into small pieces
- 1 tablespoon hemp oil or walnut oil
- Dash of tamari to serve

I work with those recovering from eating disorders, and one client of mine said that they liked the soup recipes as they had very nourishing ingredients, including essential oils which add to flavour and benefit the body. Soup is also good because it's filling without being too heavy. This velvety, creamy soup is a soothing, nourishing meal in a bowl. Drizzling over the oil provides a valuable source of omega 3 fatty acids which can often be lacking in diets.

- Christine Bailey

SWEET POTATO & PEANUT BUTTER

It sounds a strange combination, but not only is it a very quick way to get adequate carbs, proteins and fats into your meal due to the density of peanut butter, it tastes absolutely delicious. Probably the most popular thing on the menu at St Ann's!

- Phoenix Ward patients

Serves: 1
Cook Time: 60 mins

Food Groups:
carbohydrate

Ingredients:

- 300 - 400g sweet potato
- 1 tablespoon peanut butter

Instructions:

Bake sweet potato at oven to 180°C. for 60 minutes or until done.

Slice open and fluff insides of potato.

Add a tablespoon of peanut butter and mix well within the skin. Serve.

CHICKEN GRABBERS

I don't like cabbage or pepper but know I should eat a range of veggies. I adapted this recipe years ago from a recipe book making it simpler. I'm a bit of a grab a handful of this kind of girl and don't have the time or inclination to make fancy food. This is now my favourite all time recipe and we have it most weeks, I love the sauce, garlic, chilli and ginger - mmmmmh - plus it gets some more vegetables inside me.
- Jennie Southwood

Serves: 4
Prep Time: 10 mins
Cook Time: 20 mins

Food Groups:
protein, vegetables

Instructions:

Cook the chicken thighs in a baking tray at 180 for approx.imately25 minutes or until cooked. Chop into bite sized pieces and set aside.

Throw the salad together in bowl and roughly mix with your hands.

Mix the dressing ingredients together, adding garlic and onions to taste.

At dinner time, grab a bowl, grab a handful or two of salad (literally), a spoonful or two of chicken, lavish with sauce, grab a fork and   eat.

Ingredients:

Meal

- 1/4 cabbage, shredded
- 1 - 2 carrots, julienne (matchstick strips)
- 1 red pepper, julienne
- coriander
- bunch of spring onions, sliced lengthways
- 1/2 kg chicken thighs

Dressing

- 2 glugs of olive oil
- 2 garlic cloves (minced)
- 1 large red chilli
- 1cm grated
- 1 - 2 tablespoon. balsamic vinegar
- 1 - 2 tablespoon. soy sauce
- squeeze of lemon

Chicken San Choi Bow

Serves: 4
Prep Time: 10 mins
Cook Time: 10 mins

Food Groups:
carbohydrates, vegetables, fats

Instructions:

Soak noodles in hot water for 3 - 5 minutes. Rinse with cold water then drain thoroughly.

Heat frying pan or wok over high heat. Add oil, mushroom, garlic, celery and ginger, and cook stirring for 2 minutes. Drain noodles, chop coarsely and add to pan together with water chestnuts and chicken. Cook stirring continuously for 2 minutes.

To make sauce, mix oyster sauce, soy sauce, sesame oil, dry sherry and egg in a small bowl. Add mixture to pan and cook for 5 minutes. Remove from the heat, stir through bean shoots and allow to cool a little.

Carefully separate the lettuce leaves, keeping them whole to form cups. Wash and shake dry. Fill lettuce cups with chicken mixture, top with spring onion and chilli, and drizzle with hoisin sauce.

Ingredients:

Meal

- 50 g vermicelli rice noodles
- 2 tablespoons coconut oil
- 6 - 8 shitake mushrooms, chopped
- 2 garlic cloves, finely chopped
- 2 stalks celery, finely diced
- a pinch of grated ginger
- 225 g water chestnuts, chopped
- 500 g cooked chicken, finely chopped in food processor
- 1 handful bean shoots
- 1 iceberg lettuce
- 6 spring onions, finely sliced
- 1 long red chilli, deseeded and finely chopped
- hoisin sauce to serve

Sauce

- 4 tablespoons oyster sauce
- 2 tablespoons soy sauce
- 1/2 tablespoons sesame oil
- 2 tablespoons dry sherry or Chinese wine
- 1 egg, beaten

My youngest son says he doesn't like mushrooms. When I first served him San Choi Bow, he pointed at the shitake mushroom pieces and asked, 'What is this?' I replied, 'Shitake.' The absence of 'mushroom' made all the difference. It's all in the delivery. I chop the mushrooms finely so they are not detectable. It's one of his favourite meals, but I think what he likes the most is that he gets to eat with his hands.

- Jodie Blight

Coconut Curry Wild Rice Soup

Serves: 5 - 6
Prep Time: 40 mins
Cook Time: 30 mins

Food Groups:
carbohydrates,
vegetables

Ingredients:

- 2 tablespoon olive oil
- 2 teaspoon red curry paste
- 2 large cloves garlic, minced
- 2 yellow onions, chopped
- 300g wild rice, rinsed
- 4 cups water
- 1 yellow - fleshed sweet potato, peeled and cut into cubes
- 1 ½ teaspoon fine grain sea salt
- 2 teaspoon ground turmeric
- 1 tablespoon granulated sugar
- 1 tablespoon soy sauce
- 1 can coconut milk
- juice of 1 lime

Instructions:

Heat 1 tablespoon of the olive oil in a heavy pot over medium - high heat. Add the curry paste, garlic, and onions and saute for 3 to 4 minutes, until the onion begins to soften. Mix well so that the curry paste is mixed evenly.

Add the wild rice and 3 cups of the water and stir. Bring the mixture to a simmer and then lower the heat to medium - low. Cover and cook for about 40 minutes, until tender.

Heat the remaining 1 tablespoon of olive oil in a pan over medium - high heat. Add the diced sweet potatoes and half a teaspoon of the sea salt. Toss in the olive oil and cook for several minutes until they start to brown and cook until the sweet potatoes are cooked through.

When the wild rice is tender, add the turmeric, sugar, soy sauce, coconut milk, and remaining teaspoon of sea salt. Stir, return to a simmer, and then cook for an additional 5 minutes. Remove the pot from the heat and stir in the lime juice and additional salt if needed. Serve topped with a scoop of sweet potatoes.

This is one I have every year when I travel...I've been lucky enough to find a pretty close recipe. Another name for it is Sunshine Soup!
- Michael Smith

Simple Sweet Rice

It's simple, easy, and ou can make loads and store it in plastic boxes for later. A rice cooker is probably the best invention.

- Joseph Reddington

From: Joseph Reddington

Serves: 4

Prep Time: 5 mins

Cook Time: 30 mins

Food Groups:
carbohydrates,
fruits

Ingredients:

- 300 g rice
- 400g tin of chopped pineapple
- Water
- 1 tablespoon olive oil
- Soy sauce

Instructions:

If you have a rice cooker, add all the Ingredients: and cook.

If you are using a normal plan, boil the rice for 15 - 20 minutes until almost cooked, before draining the majority of the water out.

Add the pineapple and simmer for a further 5 minutes.

Serve with a protein choice - chicken, fish and beans al work well.

STUFFED PEPPERS

I like cooking meals that can be easily adapted to what is in the fridge or store cupboard. Stuffed peppers are great for this, as anything goes! I particularly like the Mediterranean Ingredients: in this version as it reminds me of holidays past.
- Rosa Brown

Serves: 3 as starter - 6 as main

Prep Time: 20 mins

Cook Time: 45 mins

Food Groups: vegatables, dairy

Ingredients:

- 3 red peppers
- 250g feta cheese
- small red onion
- 10 - 15 sundried tomatoes
- 130g pancetta cubes
- chopped basil or parsley
- lemon juice
- 130g bread crumbs
- olive oil

Instructions:

Halve the peppers lengthways and remove all the seeds and membrane. Chop the onion and sundried tomatoes into small pieces.

Fry pancetta until golden, then drain onto kitchen paper and leave to cool

Crumble the feta into a bowl, and mix in the red onions, sundried tomatoes, herbs and pancetta. Mix well. Add lemon juice to taste.

Fill the peppers with the mixture on top with a sprinkling of breadcrumbs and drizzle of olive oil.

Bake in a preheated oven for around 45 minutes until the bread crumbs are golden.

Vegan Cheese Sauce

When I was a child, I'd regularly eat cheesey dishes that, to me, where the ultimate comfor food. This very simple béchamel really openec my eyes to vegan cooking and means I can rec reate dishes that take me straight back to m early years, at home, feet up. It means I ca make any of those dishes very easily, it' healthy and it can so easily be customized int other flavours (add pesto for a summer lasagn that pops, or pour it over some nut meat). I a ways head back to this simple core recipe fc much of my food.

- Jennifer Duke

Serves: 4
Prep Time: 5 mins
Cook Time: 15 mins

Food Groups:
Additional protein
(not a portion in
itself)

Ing.

- 500 ml soy milk (or other nut milk)
- Salt and pepper
- 3 tablespoons olive oil
- 2 tablespoons flour (gluten free also works)
- 125g nutritional yeast
- ½ teaspoon of turmeric

Instructions:

Heat a pan and melt the butter, or heat the oil, until runny. Turn the heat off, stir in the flour and nutritional yeast thoroughly, then pour in a cup of the soy milk.

Turn the heat back on and whisk thoroughly until the mixture thickens. Continue adding cups of milk and repeating the process until all the milk is used up.

Add turmeric for colour, and the salt and pepper to taste. If using as a lasagne creamy sauce, then leave a little runner as it will thicken in the oven.

Use as needed in your desired recipe.

For use on mac and cheese, cauliflower cheese, potato bake, as a lasagne cream sauce or in any case when you need a béchamel.

DINNER

CART DRIVERS SPAGHETTI

Serves: 4
Prep Time: 5 mins
Cook Time: 15 mins

Food Groups:
carbohydrates,
protein, vegetables

Ingredients:

- 25g mushrooms
- 4 tablespoon olive oil
- 1 garlic clove, crushed
- 1 onion
- 70g pack pancetta, finely chopped
- 200g can tuna in oil, drained and flaked
- 600g cherry tomatoes, quartered, or 1 400g tin of tomatoes
- Salt and freshly ground pepper
- 400g spaghetti
- cheese to serve

Instructions:

Heat the olive oil in a frying pan over a medium heat, add the onion and garlic and fry gently until soft.

Add the pancetta and allow to brown a little. Stir in the mushrooms and tuna and fry for a few minutes, then add the tomatoes and season.

Simmer for around 10 - 15 minutes, until cooked and reduced.

Meanwhile, cook the spaghetti in a large pan of boiling salted water until it is al dente. Drain and mix with the sauce.

Season with black pepper, sprinkle with (plenty of) cheese and serve.

On Monday evenings Mum used to take us to swimming lessons, leaving Dad to cook dinner. One night he surprised us all with this delicious pasta dish that he had seen on a cooking programme. Buoyed by his success and our demands for a repeat of the meal, Dad started to be more creative. Over time it developed, Dad chucking in whatever ingredients he had handy, and renaming it 'Bicycle Riders Fusilli' or 'Lorry Drivers Macaroni' some variation on the theme anyway. This version of spaghetti alla carrettiera is by far the best.

- Michael Baker

VEGETABLE CRUMBLE

This is something homely my Mum always used to make, especially in the autumn/winter when you have quite a few vegetables lying around and want a quick, one - pot dish. Its so easy and tasty, its wowed my vegetarian friends and converted even the most determined meat eater too!
- John Linkins

Serves: 4
Prep Time: 20 mins
Cook Time: 30 mins

Food Groups:
carbohydrates, vegetables

Ingredients:

Meal

- 200g onions
- 200g celery
- 200g butternut squash
- 100g peas
- 3/4 pint vegetable stock
- 2 teaspoon coriander
- 2 teaspoon cumin
- 1 teaspoon tumeric
- 1 teaspoon chilli
- garlic and herbs

Topping

- 10g wholewheat flour
- 70g butter
- 100g oats
- 70g cheese

Instructions:

Preheat oven to 180°C. Cook vegetables (other than the peas) together in a pan with a little oil/butter. Add spices and stock

Add peas and leave to simmer for 10 minutes until the liquid begins to reduce.

Make crumble topping by rubbing together flour and butter, then add the oats and half the cheese.

Put the vegetable mixture in an ovenproof dish and sprinkle the topping over.

Sprinkle the rest of the cheese over the top of the crumble and bake for 20 - 30 minutes until brown and the filling is just bubbling up.

Fish pie with Swede & Potato

This is a complete, nutritious meal in one pot. It can transform even the cheapest fish into a delicious meal.

- Thereza Baker

Serves: 4
Prep Time: 40 mins
Cook Time: 30 mins

Food Groups:
protein,
carbohydrates

Ingredients:

- 500g floury potatoes, cut into chunks
- 1 medium swede (weighing about 600g), cut into chunks
- 200g tub soft cheese with garlic and herbs
- 150ml vegetable stock
- 4 teaspoon cornflour, blended with 2 tablespoon cold water
- 650g skinless, boneless white fish, cut into large chunks
- 100g cooked peeled prawns
- 1 teaspoon chopped fresh parsley

Instructions:

Preheat the oven to 190°C. Cook the potatoes and swede in boiling water until tender (about 20 minutes).

While the potatoes and swede cook, put the soft cheese and stock into a large saucepan and heat gently, stirring with a wooden spoon, until blended and smooth. Now add the blended cornflour and cook until thick.

Stir the fish into the sauce with the prawns and parsley. Season with some pepper.

Tip the mixture into a baking dish. Drain the potatoes and swede, mash them well and season with black pepper. Spoon the mash over the fish to cover it completely.

Bake for 25 - 30 minutes until piping hot, then transfer to a hot grill for a few minutes to brown the top.

The Vietnamese Chicken Curry That Made Sarah Cry

Serves: 6
Prep Time: 20 mins
Cook Time: 10 hours

Food Groups:
protein,
carbohydrates,
vegetables

Instructions:

Place the chicken, lemongrass, garlic, ginger, fish sauce and half the curry powder or paste into the slow cooker insert. Toss to combine. Cover and refrigerate for at least an hour orovernight.

In the morning, place the slow cooker insert with the chicken into the slow cooker; add the remaining curry powder or paste, stock, vegetables, coconut milk, stevia, leftover lemongrass and bay leaves. Stir to combine. Cook on low for 7 - 8 hours or high for 3 - 4 hours.

If you like a thicker curry, 20 minutes before serving combine 2 - 3 tablespoons arrowroot or cornflour, mixed to a paste in cold water and pour into slow cooker. Cook on high with the lid off for 20 minutes until sauce thickens.

Garnish with shallots and serve with roti, mountain bread or pappadams.

Ingredients:

- 700g chicken pieces
- 1 stalk lemongrass, peeled and thinly sliced (only use the cream end, reserve the green end)
- 2 cloves garlic, crushed
- 3cm knob fresh ginger, grated (or 1 tablespoon store - bought minced ginger)
- 2 tablespoons fish sauce
- 50g yellow curry powder or curry paste
- 250ml chicken stock
- 2 medium sweet potatoes, cut into 2.5cm chunks
- 1 large carrot, cut into chunks
- 1x400ml can coconut milk
- 1 teaspoon sugar
- 2 bay leaves
- 2 green shallots, finely sliced
- 2 - 3 tablespoons arrowroot or cornflour, mixed to a paste in cold water
- Roti, mountain bread or pappadams to serve

When I'm asked to cite my favourite food experience, this is the one I share. I first ate cari ga on a mountain - bike trip with my brother Pete in Vietnam. We'd been riding for nine hours through a desert and one of the highest mountains in the country, plus I had food poisoning. By the time I arrived, I was dead set delirious and my brother found us the closest hole in the wall place steaming with a caldron of this Vietnamese version of chicken curry. At the first spoonful, I cried. Then I ordered two more servings.
                    - Sarah Wilson

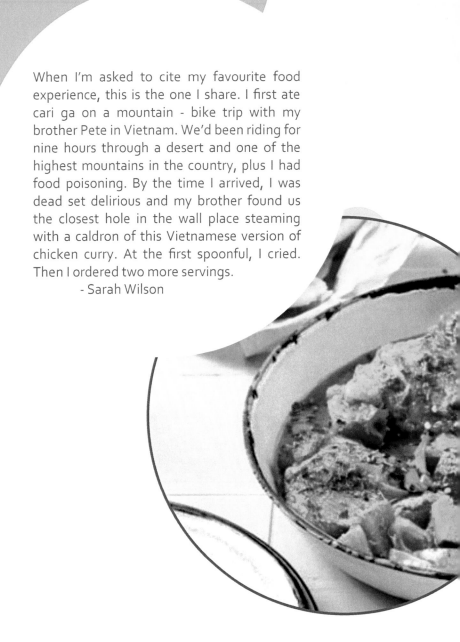

Beef & Bacon Stir Fry

It's easy and delicious, and can be made with any meat.
- Jimmy Eckersley

Serves: 2
Prep Time: 20 mins
Cook Time: 30 mins

Food Groups:
carbohydrates, vegetables, protein

Ingredients:

- 160g lean beef
- spring onions
- green pepper
- 1 can of water chestnuts
- 1 cove of garlic
- 1 onion
- 2 tomatoes
- black pepper
- salt
- 3 tablespoons butter
- 300g bean sprouts
- soy sauce
- 2 rashers of lean bacon
- 150g rice
- sugar

Instructions:

Put on the rice to cook for 20 - 30 minutes.

Slice the beef into thin strips, chop the bacon into squares, cut up the spring onions, green pepper and onion and drain the water chestnuts and dice.

Cover tomatoes with water in a bowl, microwave for 90 seconds and then skin and chop.

Put 2 tablespoon of butter into a wok, heat with salt, black pepper and garlic. When melted add strips chicken and colour for 10 minutes or until it is done. Add the bacon and cook for 5 minutes. Add 1 tablespoon of sugar and soy sauce to taste.

Add chopped tomatoes to the chicken and bacon and stir. If you need extra tomato, use tomato puree. Add green peppers, onions, water chestnuts and spring onions.

Add the cooked rice, stir and cover and put on a low heat.

Veggie Chilli

When I was growing up, my parents ran a pub which we also lived in, we became locally famous for our chilli con carne, so I think chilli has always been in my blood. Being the only vegetarian in a carnivorous household my dad taught me how to make this recipe just before I left for university, and it remains a favourite.

- Charlotte Maughan –Jones

Serves: 4
Prep Time: 10 mins
Cook Time: 45 mins

Food Groups:
protein, vegetables, fats

Ingredients:

- 375g all purpose flour
- 500g vegetarian mince (quorn)
- 400g tin kidney beans
- 2 red onions
- 2 cloves of garlic
- 2 cans of chopped tomatoes
- 1 small jar of sundried tomatoes
- 1 - 2 teaspoon of dried chilli flakes
- 1 tablespoon of rapeseed or olive oil
- cheese to taste
- 300g rice

Instructions:

Chop the onion and crush the garlic and fry in the oil for a few minutes until soft, but not browned.

In the meantime place all the sundries tomatoes into a blender and blend into a paste. Add this paste to the onion and garlic and fry for a few minutes.

Add the chilli flakes (to taste, I have a sensitive tongue so use no more than 1 teaspoon, but you may require more or less than this) and stir.

Add the vegetarian mince and stir until mixed with the rest of the Ingredients:.

Add the tomatoes and bring to the boil. Reduce to a simmer and simmer for half an hour.

Add the kidney beans and cook for a further 5 - 10minutes until soft but not mushy. (The beans can be added at the same time as the tomatoes, but I find they become very mushy, and I prefer them a bit firmer).

Serve with boiled rice and a sprinkle of grated cheese on top.

Chicken Chasseur

My sister came home from Australia last summer, she is an amazing cook and taught me how to make this dish. I've eaten it a lot since I started to recover as it is healthy and wholesome and very very tasty.

- Ruby Tuesday

Serves: 2
Prep Time: 20 mins
Cook Time: 60 mins

Food Groups:
protein, vegetables

Ingredients:

- 2 chicken breasts
- 1 onion
- 1 clove of garlic
- 4 carrots
- I teablespoon of tomato puree
- beef stock cube
- Worcester Sauce to taste

Instructions:

Cut 2 chicken breasts in to chunks and fry in a pot over a medium heat until just done.

When the chicken is done, remove it from the pot and place on a clean plate.

Next fry chopped onions, garlic, mushrooms and carrots in the same pot.

Add a dollop of tomato purée and stir for two minutes.

Return the chicken to the pot, and add the beef stock cube with enough water to cover the chicken and vegetables.

Next, add a dash of Worchester sauce. Taste and adjust seasoning.

Let it bubble away for as long as possible. The longer you leave it, the better it will taste.

Serve with potatoes.

QUICK & EASY SALMON PASTA

I ripped this out of a magazine years ago. I just like to include a bit of fish in my diet and this is such a simple way to do so, - plus it contains green veg and carbs to keep you going!
- John Linkins

Serves: 4
Prep Time: 20 mins
Cook Time: 20 mins

Food Groups:
carbohydrates, protein, fats, vegetables

Ingredients:

- 300g wholewheat Pasta
- 350g broccoli/peas/spinach
- 300g salmon
- 150g Philadelphia (or other soft cheese) with herbs
- 150ml low fat yoghurt
- 2 tablespoons sun - dried tomato puree

Instructions:

Cook pasta and veg in one pan for 12 mins

Poach salmon in another, for 15-20 mins.

Mix up soft cheese, yogurt and paste.

Drain salmon and cool.

Drain pasta, crumble in salmon and add cheese mixture.

Enjoy hot or cold!

Apricot Glazed Chicken

Serves: 2
Prep Time: 15 mins
Cook Time: 60 mins

Food Groups:
protein,
carbohydrates,
vegetables, fats

Ingredients:

- 2 tablespoons sunflower oil
- 2 tablespoon. butter
- drizzle of olive oil
- 1 bunch rosemary (chopped)
- 1 bunch chives (chopped)
- salt
- pepper
- 500g roasting potatoes
- 3 carrots
- 2 yellow onions
- 2 chicken breasts
- 1 jar of apricot preserves

Instructions:

Preheat oven to 200 °C.

Chop potatoes, carrots and onions and put in large roasting pan.

Lightly toss with olive oil. Season with salt and pepper. Place chicken over cut veggies.

Melt 2 tablespoon. of butter in pan, add to that some chopped Rosemary and chopped chives. Pour over chicken and vegetables.

Bake for about 45 minutes.

When the chicken are browning, melt some apricot preserves in the same butter pan and pour over the chicken. Cook for another ten minutes and serve with potatoes.

Growing up my mother always cooked. I have lovely memories of the lunches she packed me and the yummy dinners she served my family. She taught me how to cook and I have some wonderful memories of us in our kitchen. Unfortunately, when I was 12 years old, she was diagnosed with Multiple Sclerosis and her ability to do regular activities became very difficult. It was at this time that I started to get ill with an eating disorder, and while my journey had its ups and downs, I was finally able to find recovery. My mother, on the other hand, was not so lucky, as her decline was devastating and she passed away. When I was 22, I met my current husband and felt my luck turn around. Not only was he caring, supportive and thoughtful but he also had a family that treated me like their own. I was (and still am) especially touched by the way his mother embraced me. A fantastic cook herself, she shares many of her recipes with me and we discuss tricks of the trade often. One of my favorites is an Apricot Glazed Chicken, which I made for my husband the first time we celebrated his birthday together. This dish reminds me that although I have experienced hardships, my life is ripe with sweetness. When I make this dish today, I remember the beginning of my relationship with my husband and how much we have grown together. I also feel so blessed to have built such a strong bond with my mother in law. May this recipe bring love into your home as well :)

- Maxine

Handmade Pasta

Serves: 1
Prep Time: 45 mins
Cook Time: 5 mins

Food Groups:
carbohydrates

Ingredients:

Quantity per person

- 100 g of 'oo' flour (super fine flour used for pasta, you can find this in most supermarkets)
- 1 medium sized egg (45 - 50 g)
- 1 teaspoon of extra virgin olive oil

Instructions:

Measure out flour required, and place on a flat, clean surface. Make a big well in the centre of the pile of flour.

Add the eggs, one at a time and slowly stir to combine in the flour gradually. Progressively add the olive oil to the flour mixture, one teaspoon at a time, as you add the egg.

Once the flour, egg, and oil has combined to form a dough, start kneading the dough for 10-15 minutes (knead dough by pulling the dough into the centre with your fingers and gently but firmly press down with the palm of your hand into the centre of the dough. Turn the dough 90 degrees, and continue to use the same motion). If you find the dough a little dry, add a bit more extra virgin olive oil, as required.

Wrap dough in cling wrap or place under a wet towel and let it rest for 10-15 minutes. After resting, take it out and lightly press the centre - it should spring back up, which indicates that the dough is ready for rolling into pasta sheets.

Roll the pasta out into thin sheets and slice into parpedelle strips - about 2cm wide.

Boil a big pot of water with a spoon of salt, and cook pasta Once the water boils, put some of the pasta into the water and cook for 4-5 minutes, or until it starts floating to the top.

BOLOGNESE SAUCE

This recipe is inspired by handmade pasta cooking lessons I experienced while I was visiting Florence. Handmade pasta is actually quite simple in terms of ingredients, but the magic happens in the 'labour of love' of kneading and rolling out the pasta. If you haven't tried the taste of hand made, fresh pasta before, give it a go. Even though it requires some effort, it's worth it! It's also a great way to catch up with friends/family by enjoying the experience and fun of making pasta together. People discover the world through food - it's a way to explore and connect with the world around you.

- Tu Dinh Tran

Serves: 5
Prep Time: 10 mins
Cook Time: 45 mins

Food Groups:
protein, vegetables

Ingredients:

- 1 large onion (diced)
- 550 g of minced beef
- 550 g canned tomatoes
- 4 cloves of sliced garlic
- 6 tablespoon of extra virgin olive oil
- 300 ml of red wine
- 1 small bunch of basil
- 1 teaspoon of chilli flakes or fresh chilli
- salt & pepper
- Parmesan cheese - grated/shredded

Instructions:

Heat the oil in a large, deep frying pan, add garlic and onion and continue to stir fry until onions are caramelised.

Add minced beef and continue to fry until meat has browned. Add tomatoes and basil and let it cook for 5 minutes. After 5 minutes, use a wooden spoon to break up the whole tomatoes.

Add red wine and cook through until you can't smell the alcohol from the wine anymore.

Cook on medium heat for 10 - 15 minutes, stir occasionally, add the chilli.

Pour over your pasta, and add parmesan, salt and pepper, as required.

Chicken & Vegetable Paella de Orti

I saw my dad make this meal every Sunday in summer. Always in the same place, slow, focussed, constantly assessing the water, the salt, the rice, cooking for the family that he build and loved. Paella is a social event, a family event, an excuse to be together....and my dad made a cracking succulent excuse! Now it's our time to take that role. His children and grandchildren miss his paellas. It's our time to continue building the family traditions that he started.

- Javier Orti

Serves: 8 - 10
Prep Time: 20 mins
Cook Time: 90 mins

Food Groups:
carbohydrates,
protein, vegetables

Ingredients:

- 1 kg rice
- 1 kg chicken
- 1/2 red bell pepper
- 1/2 green pepper
- 1 bag of frozen vegetables
- 1 fresh tomato cut into small squares
- 2 cloves garlic (minced)
- 1 medium onion (chopped)
- salt
- saffron
- olive oil
- rosemary
- lemon Juice
- 6 - 7 litres of water

Instructions:

Oil the bottom of the pan and fry the chicken thrown into the pan over a high heat. Once fried on both sides, take it out of the pan and put it aside.

Reduce the heat and fry the vegetables together with the onion and garlic, then the tomato.

Re - add the chicken, and fill the pan with water. Add in the rosemary.

Let it boil over medium heat, until the water has reduced by half. Then refill and let it boil again. Add seasoning to taste.

Let it simmer about 20 minutes, always over medium heat.

Add the rice, and boil for 18 - 20 minutes, adding water if necessary, before dashing with lemon juice.

Multi Bean & Chorizo Stew with Tortilla Shards

Chunky, hearty and with a little kick! Leftovers can be chilled for lunch or frozen and kept for a rainy day.

- Jami eMalcolm

Serves: 4
Prep Time: 10 mins
Cook Time: 30 mins

Food Groups:
carbohydrates, protein, vegetables

Ingredients:

- 400g tin mixed bean
- 400g tin butterbeans
- 400g chopped tomatoes
- chilli to taste
- 225 g chopped chorizo
- red pepper
- red onion
- spinach - handful
- 2 large tortillas

Instructions:

Start by frying the chorizo, pepper and onion in a big pan for 5 minutes until softened. The chorizo releases oil so you don't need any.

Add both tins, tomatoes, half a can of water and whatever seasoning you wish.

Cover with a lid and let it simmer for at least 20 minutes on a low heat.

You can add the spinach 2 minutes before the end until it has wilted.

After you add the spinach dab each side of the tortillas with water and grill until hardened.

Cut the tortillas into 8 to 10 pieces and use to scoop up the stew!

Aloo Gobi Salmon Curry

This curry is full of flavour and highly nutritious. Good enough to serve at a dinner party!

- Laurel Alper

Serves: 2
Prep Time: 10 mins
Cook Time: 30 mins

Food Groups: carbohydrates, protein, vegetables, dairy

Ingredients:

- 2 skinned salmon fillets
- 4 cauliflower florets
- 1 large onion
- 2 handfuls of flat, de - stalked and quartered mushrooms
- 2 pressed garlic cloves
- Finely chopped chilli
- 1 teaspoon cumin seeds
- 1 teaspoon turmeric
- 1 teaspoon salt
- handful of chopped coriander
- 8 - 10 new potatoes

Instructions:

In a saucepan bring the potato and cauliflower to the boil, then simmer for 15 - 20 minutes until cooked.

Meanwhile, add ½ inch of water to frying pan then add onions, garlic, chilli, cumin seeds, turmeric and salt.

Cook onions till softened and nicely browning.

Then add salmon fillets to frying pan (skin - side up) and coat with curry sauce.

Cook for 6-8 minutes then add mushrooms . Turn salmon fillets over and cook for further 6-8 minutes.

Drain potatoes and cauliflower and quarter potatoes.

Just as salmon is ready, add potatoes and cauliflower florets and coat in sauce.

Cook for a minute or two more.

Kosho Mangsho - Lamb Curry

It's easy, and tasty. I made it for my housewarming party and my family loved it! And I can't cook....
- Catherine Cowie

Serves: 4
Prep Time: 2 hours
Cook Time: 50 mins

Food Groups:
protein, vegetables

Instructions:

Marinate the lamb in the spices, and refrigerate overnight or for at least 2 hours. Take lamb out of the fridge and bring to room temperature.

Heat pressure cooker over medium - high heat and add butter or oil. When oil is hot, stir - fry onions until translucent then add lamb. Stir well and simmer until juices are released.

Simmer on medium heat for 40 minutes & remove from heat.

Adjust salt to taste and stir in garam masala.

Serve with potatoes, Indian bread or steamed basmati rice.

Ingredients:

- 500g lamb cut into medium chunks
- 200g plain yogurt
- 1 tablespoon turmeric
- 2 tablespoon butter
- 2 large onions chopped
- 2 tablespoon ginger paste
- 2 tablespoon garlic paste
- 1 tablespoon garam masala
- 3 teaspoon cumin powder
- 4 teaspoon coriander powder
- 1 teaspoon red chilli powder
- 2 large tomatoes chopped

Chicken Noodles

Serves: 3
Prep Time: 15 mins
Cook Time: 50 mins

Food Groups:
carbohydrates,
protein, vegetables

Ingredients:

- 3 chicken legs or breasts
- 750ml water
- 500ml chicken broth
- 1 teaspoon dried thyme
- 2 bay leaves
- salt & pepper
- 1 large onion, chopped
- 4 carrots, peeled & chopped
- 2 ribs celery, chopped
- 400g egg noodles
- 100g frozen peas
- 200ml milk
- 2 Tablespoons flour

Instructions:

Place chicken in the bottom of a large heavy - bottomed pot. Add water, chicken broth, dried thyme, bay leaves, salt, pepper, onion, carrots, and celery.

Bring to a boil then place a lid on top, lower heat, and simmer for 30 minutes, or until chicken is cooked through. Remove chicken from pot then shred and set aside.

Meanwhile, add egg noodles to pot and cook according to package directions. Once tender, stir in peas. In a separate container with a screw - top lid, combine milk and flour then shake to combine. Drizzle into Dutch oven then stir to combine.

Cook for 3 - 4 minutes or until mixture is thick and bubbly. Add chicken back to the pot then taste and add more salt & pepper if necessary. Let chicken & noodles sit for 10 minutes to thicken before serving.

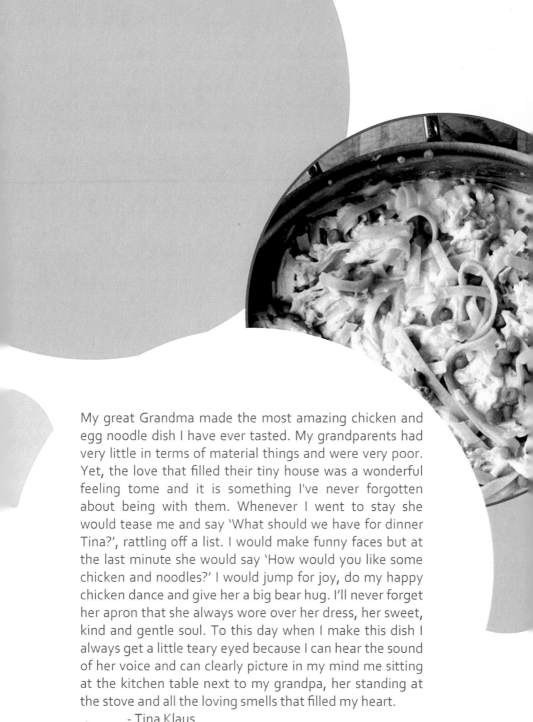

My great Grandma made the most amazing chicken and egg noodle dish I have ever tasted. My grandparents had very little in terms of material things and were very poor. Yet, the love that filled their tiny house was a wonderful feeling tome and it is something I've never forgotten about being with them. Whenever I went to stay she would tease me and say 'What should we have for dinner Tina?', rattling off a list. I would make funny faces but at the last minute she would say 'How would you like some chicken and noodles?' I would jump for joy, do my happy chicken dance and give her a big bear hug. I'll never forget her apron that she always wore over her dress, her sweet, kind and gentle soul. To this day when I make this dish I always get a little teary eyed because I can hear the sound of her voice and can clearly picture in my mind me sitting at the kitchen table next to my grandpa, her standing at the stove and all the loving smells that filled my heart.

  - Tina Klaus

Pork in Marsala & Red Wine

This recipe is from my mother - in - law, Jean. She is 100% Italian and a fabulous cook - my husband is one of three boys, and they loved good food! Her pork chops are a favourite in our own household, and reminds us of being back home. Needless to say, this dish pairs well with pasta.

- Dana Bisenius

Serves: 4
Prep Time: 10 mins
Cook Time: 70 mins

Food Groups:
protein, fats

Ingredients:

- 75ml olive oil
- 1tablespoon butter
- 4 pork chops, trimmed of any fat and pounded thin
- 60g flour spread on a plate
- 1 teaspoon chopped garlic
- 1 tablespoon tomato paste dissolved in 250ml red wine
- pinch of fennel seeds
- 1 tablespoon chopped parsley
- salt
- pepper

Instructions:

Dissolve tomato paste in marsala and red wine, put aside.

Dredge chops in flour (after absorbing excess moisture with paper towels) Heat oil and butter in pan on medium. Add chops, and brown on both sides.

Add garlic to butter and meat.

Just after garlic browns, add the wine mix.

Season with salt and pepper, and add fennel seeds.

When wine has bubbled for one minute, cover tightly and simmer at a lower heat. Cook 1 hour or until tender, turning occasionally.

Mix in parsley just before serving.

TERIYAKI PORK

This recipe couldn't be more simple. I'm a food writer, chef, competitive French fry eater, and owner of one too many frilly aprons, and on my website I share my recipes for healthy hedonism and tips on living a more balanced life .
- Phoebe Labine

Serves: 2
Prep Time: 20 mins + overnight
Cook Time: 30 mins

Food Groups:
protein,
carbohydrates

Ingredients:

- 100ml organic maple syrup
- 100ml tamari
- 2 large garlic cloves, minced
- 2 inches fresh ginger root
- 400g pork or chicken
- 100g rice

Instructions:

In a small food processor, puree the maple syrup, tamari, garlic, and ginger until smooth. Alternatively, you can mind the ginger and garlic by hand and whisk in the rremaining I=ingredients.

Transfer the marinade to a resealable plastic bag. Add the meat and swish around until coated. Marinate in the refrigerator for at least an hour, preferably overnight.

Preheat the oven to 250°C. Remove the pork from the marinade and set on a foil - lined baking sheet.

Roast in the oven for approximately 20 minutes, until the pork is nicely browned on top. Allow to rest on a cutting board for 10 minutes. At the same time, cook 50g rice per person.

Meanwhile, transfer the remaining marinade to a small saucepan. Cook on medium heat until reduced by half.

Slice the pork on the bias, drizzle with the reduced sauce, and serve immediately with a side of with rice.

Sweet Potato Bisque

Serves: 4
Prep Time: 20 mins
Cook Time: 30 mins

Food Groups:
vegetables

Instructions:

Heat oil in a large pot then saute onions until softened but not browned.

Stir in broth, sweet potatoes, ginger, thyme, allspice, and crushed red pepper. Bring to a boil over light heat. Reduce heat and simmer uncovered, stirring occasionally, until potatoes are just tender (about 8 minutes).

Scoop 3 heaped cups of the veggies and 1 cup broth into a blender (or food processor) and puree. Return mixture to the pot.

Combine 2/3 of the canned tomatoes and the peanut butter in the blender and puree.

Mix this into the pot and add remaining tomatoes.

Bring the entire mixture to a simmer for 3 - 5 more minutes until piping hot. Salt and pepper to taste, garnish and serve.

Ingredients:

Meal

- 2 tablespoon olive oil
- 2 large onions, diced
- 1.5 - 2 l vegetable broth
- 1.5 - 2 kg sweet potatoes, peeled and cubed
- 2 tablespoons fresh ginger, peeled and minced
- 2 teaspoons dried thyme leaves
- 2 teaspoons dried allspice
- 400g can crushed tomatoes
- 150G smooth peanut butter
- 1/4 - 1/2 teaspoon hot red pepper flakes (to taste)
- salt and pepper to taste

Garnishes

- sour cream or plain yogurt
- sunflower or pumpkin seeds
- fresh parsley

I love this soup! The taste, texture, colour and aroma are both energizing and calming and it has deep significance for me. My mother found it as we were planning my first retreat in 2013. Both my mom, daughter and sister helped do the food for that event and the women who attended fell in love with the dish. Now we include it in every retreat and workshop. This soup is healing in so many ways. Nutritionally, it provides a nice balance, it's warm, and it is a very grounding food helping decrease anxiety and get us present in our bodies. I hope you enjoy making and nurturing your body and soul with this yummy meal!
- Julia Norman

Granny's Macaroni Cheese

Serves: **2**
Prep Time: **20 mins**
Cook Time: **70 minutes**

Food Groups: **protein, carbohydrates, fats, dairy**

Ingredients:

- 500 g macaroni
- 2 teaspoon salt
- 2 teaspoon olive oil
- 1 large tomato
- 1 teaspoon butter
- 1 tin tomato/onion mix or fresh tomato/onion
- 1 teaspoon sweet basil or fresh basil leaves
- pinch teaspoon onion salt
- 2 teaspoon tomato sauce
- 1 teaspoon sugar
- 500ml milk
- 2 eggs
- 1 teaspoon mustard powder
- 1teaspoon vinegar
- 1 packet cheddar cheese
- 2 teaspoon black pepper

Instructions:

Preheat oven to 180°C. Cook macaroni for 10 minutes in boiling water with two teaspoons salt and 2 teaspoons olive oil. Drain.

Fry one large tomato in butter. When soft add tomato and onion and cook slowly for a few minutes. Sprinkle with basil, salt, tomato sauce and sugar.

Mix 500ml milk with two beaten eggs and 1 teaspoon mustard powder mixed with little vinegar. Butter a big deepish pie dish (I use two smaller ones and freeze one dish uncooked to use another time).

Put layer of macaroni then tomato/onion mix and grated strong Cheddar cheese, sprinkle black pepper and then another layer of macaroni and more cheese. Sprinkle with black pepper. Pour milk mixture over and put dabs of butter on top.

Bake approximately one hour at 180 degrees uncovered.

As a child, whenever I visited my granny, she made my sister and I her macaroni and cheese as a treat. Throughout my time with an eating disorder the cheesy, oniony, sweet tomato flavours and the crispy macaroni on top became mere memories. But even then I thought of this dish lovingly, as comfort food and because it was my granny's recipe. I chose this particular recipe because many of the ingredients were high up on my "forbidden" list. Over the years, since I started recovery fifteen years ago, my granny has continued to make me this dish on occasion, when I visit her, and I love it just the same every time. Especially slathered with tomato sauce! A few months ago, I asked her for the recipe to cook for my son. I dared to make it, albeit a more modern, healthier version using organic, fresh produce. Well my son loved it and I loved it as it tasted just like my granny's macaroni and reminded me of her.

- Shani Raviv

SWEETS & PUDDINGS

'EATON MESS'

A deceptively simple dessert that anyone can make.
- Francesca Baker

Serves: 4
Prep Time: 3 mins
Cook Time: 0 mins

Food Groups:
fruits, sugars

Ingredients:

- 4 meringues
- 400g yoghurt
- 400g frozen berries

Instructions:

In individual glasses or bowls, divide the meringues evenly. With a fork, slightly crush the meringues.

Defrost the berries for a minute in the microwave. Divide them equally in the glasses and pour over yoghurt.

Flourless Pomegranate and Coconut Brownies

Serves: 8 - 12
Prep Time: 20 mins
Cook Time: 20 mins + 10 mins

Food Groups: sugars, fats

Ingredients:

Cakes

- 65g self raising flour
- 65g margarine, cut into small pieces
- 65g caster sugar
- 1 egg
- 1 teaspoon vanilla extract
- 1 teaspoon ground cinnamon
- At least 2 tablespoons of crystallised ginger finely chopped

Instructions:

Preheat oven to 180°c and place cupcake cases on a baking tray.

Place the flour, margarine, sugar, egg, vanilla, cinnamon and ginger in an electronic mixer and blend together until smooth.

Using a teaspoon, fill the cake cases to about half level with the mixture.

Bake in the oven for around 20 minutes or until golden, with a sponge that springs back when pressed. You could also try inserting a fine skewer into a cake to check if they are baked through – if the skewer comes out clean then they are okay!

Remove cakes from the oven once baked and place them on a cooling rack.

Once cool, cut a circular section from the top of the cakes and cut these in half. Fill the hole with a good teaspoon (or two!) of the ginger conserve, then place the cut out pieces on top to make the butterfly wings.

You could also add some buttercream on top of the conserve if you wish, or just enjoy as they are!

Some days call for brownies. I've long believed that chocolate is good for morale. So I present to you some that will work for a good smattering of folk. These brownies were designed during a pit dark week that involved an overseas spouse, a broken car and a teething toddler with a stomach flu. Luckily these emergency mood boosts can be muddled together in a blender quick smart. They have the pleasing flavour and texture that's a little like a fudgy coconut rough, while the antioxidant shot from the pomegranate juice and dried cranberries offers plenty of perky enthusiasm. The shards of coconut over the top aren't essential, but they do add another toasty contrast and make them look rather fetching. I tend to make one batch for me and one to freeze - that way I know a better day is never far away.

- Tori Haschka

HEAVENLY ALMOND BREAD

> Enjoy your food, and remember, you are special and worthy!
> - Nikki Du Bose

Serves: 4
Prep Time: 20 mins
Cook Time: 55 mins

Food Groups:
carbohydrates

Ingredients:

- 300g almond meal/flour
- 1/2 teaspoon baking soda
- 3 eggs
- 1 tablespoon honey
- 1/2 teaspoon apple cider vinegar
- olive oil spray/butter

For topping:
- Ginger conserve

Instructions:

Preheat the oven to 150°C.

In a big bowl mix together the almond meal/flour and baking soda.

In a medium bowl beat the eggs then add the honey and apple cider vinegar.

Now add the wet ingredients into the dry ones and mix well.

Spray a baby loaf pan with olive oil spray and pour the batter evenly into it.

Bake for 45 - 55 minutes or until a toothpick comes out clean.

Let the bread cool completely before serving.

SUPERFOOD TRUFFLES

I'm passionate about people's health and love of real food. These little chocolate nuggets are packed with super foods designed to nourish and energise the body.
- Christine Bailey

Serves: 4 - 6
Prep Time: 10 mins
Cook Time: 4 hours chill time

Food Groups:
sugars, fats, protein

Instructions:

Place the cashew nut butter, maple syrup, cacao powder and melted cacao butter in a food processor and combine. Add the remaining ingredients and process to form a dough. Chill in the fridge for about 4 hours until firm. Alternatively place in a freezer to firm up.

When the mixture is firm use a spoon to scoop out walnut size balls. Roll into balls and place on a sheet of baking parchment. Roll the truffles in a little shredded coconut, crushed pistachios or dust with cacao powder.

Ingredients:

- 115g cashew or almond nut butter
- 70g maple syrup or honey
- 2 tablespoon cacao powder to taste
- 60g melted cacao butter or dark chocolate
- 30g cup goji berries or dried cherries soaked in water for 30 mins then drained
- 2teaspoon maca powder
- Pinch of sea salt
- ½ teaspoon. vanilla extract
- 1 teaspoon ground cinnamon
- 30g shelled hemp seeds
- 30g dried cherries

Rum Balls

These are an old favourite sweet recipe from childhood, so I have a very distinct memory of how they are meant to taste. I was given a recipe challenge to make them 'healthier' and so created a version with oats, dates and vanilla. However, that memory of what the original recipe tasted life was so strong that my new version was a major disappointment and it just left me wanting the real deal more. Which of course led me to make a batch! This was the turning point for me in realising how futile "healthifying" foods that we enjoy is and how important it is to enjoy ALL foods without judgement.

- Nina Mills

Serves: 4
Prep Time: 30 mins
Cook Time: 1 hour chill time

Food Groups:
sugars

Ingredients:

- 300g almond meal/flour
- 1 packet Rich Tea biscuits
- 395g tin sweetened condensed milk
- 2 tablespoons cocoa
- 125g desiccated coconut
- Extra desiccated coconut for rolling

Instructions:

Blitz the biscuits in a food processor until they resemble biscuit crumbs (they can be a bit chunky).

In a bowl add the biscuit crumbs, sweetened condensed milk, cocoa and coconut and mix well.

Take spoonfuls of the crumb and squash to form a blob, and then roll into balls.

Toss balls through the extra coconut to coat.

Chill in the fridge for an hour.

Blueberry Oat Cake

Someone's relationship with food in my opinion is far more important than what they eat. When someone becomes relaxed around food and gives themselves permission to eat whatever they want, they naturally start to listen to their body. Sugar is crucial to the functioning of all our cells, and whether this comes in the form of honey, or as carrot, depends on the situation. No pangs of remorse. No beating yourself up. Just enjoy with gusto because it's healthy food made in the tastiest way.
- Chris Sandel

Serves: 8
Prep Time: 15 mins
Cook Time: 45 mins

Food Groups:
sugars, fats, protein

Ingredients:

- 100g wholemeal or spelt flour
- 90g oats
- 2 teaspoons baking powder
- Pinch of salt
- 1 teaspoon cinnamon
- 100g honey
- 150g plain yoghurt
- 1 tablespoon lemon juice 60 ml whole milk
- 2 medium eggs
- 150g blueberries

Instructions:

Preheat oven to 170°C. Line the bottom of a cake pan with baking parchment and grease the sides with butter.

In a mixing bowl, stir together flour, oatmeal, baking powder, salt and cinnamon.

In a separate bowl, pour in the honey, yoghurt, and lemon juice. Whisk to combine. Add milk and eggs and continue whisking until well mixed. Pour yoghurt into oats mixture and beat together until well blended. Gently stir in the blueberries until just combined.

Spoon into a cake pan and bake for 35-45 minutes. When a toothpick inserted in the centre comes out clean, the cake is done.

Ginger & Cinnamon Butterfly Cakes

erves: 2

Prep Time: 20 mins

Cook Time: 20 mins +
10 mins

Food Groups:
sugars, fats, fruit

Ingredients:

- 60 ml pomegranate juice
- 100 g pitted dates
- 4 tablespoon coconut oil (or melted butter)
- 1 ripe banana
- 4 eggs
- 40 g desiccated coconut
- 30 g coconut flour
- 50 g cocoa powder
- Pinch salt
- 50 g dried cherries, or dried cranberries
- 1 large handful coconut shards (optional)

Instructions:

Preheat the oven to 180°C and line a baking pan the size of an A4 sheet of paper with greaseproof paper.

Combine the juice, pitted dates and coconut oil in a blender. Blitz until you have a smooth, sweet slurry.

Add the banana and blend to combine. Then add the eggs and blend, followed by the desiccated coconut, coconut flour and cocoa and blend again. Finally fold through the dried fruit and transfer batter to the prepared pan.

Sprinkle the top with the coconut shards.

Bake for 20 minutes, until the coconut shards are toasted and a skewer comes out with just a few fudgy crumbs on it. Allow to cool in the tin for 10 minutes, then cut into bars or small squares.

Either eat warm, or allow to cool. These will keep well in the fridge for up to 6 days.

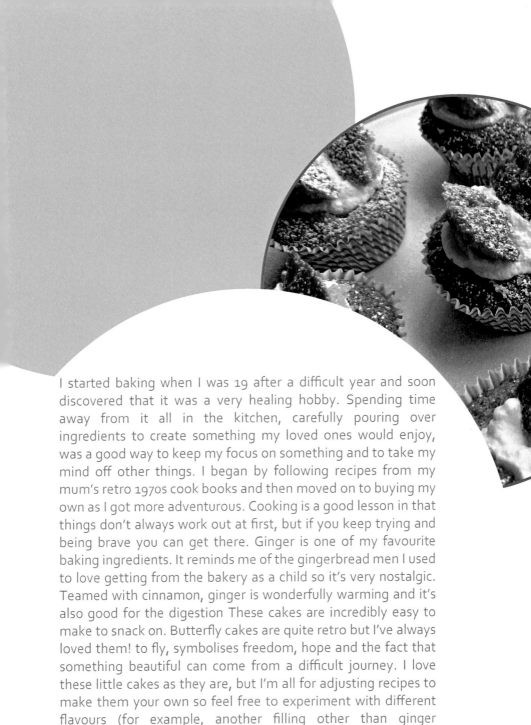

I started baking when I was 19 after a difficult year and soon discovered that it was a very healing hobby. Spending time away from it all in the kitchen, carefully pouring over ingredients to create something my loved ones would enjoy, was a good way to keep my focus on something and to take my mind off other things. I began by following recipes from my mum's retro 1970s cook books and then moved on to buying my own as I got more adventurous. Cooking is a good lesson in that things don't always work out at first, but if you keep trying and being brave you can get there. Ginger is one of my favourite baking ingredients. It reminds me of the gingerbread men I used to love getting from the bakery as a child so it's very nostalgic. Teamed with cinnamon, ginger is wonderfully warming and it's also good for the digestion These cakes are incredibly easy to make to snack on. Butterfly cakes are quite retro but I've always loved them! to fly, symbolises freedom, hope and the fact that something beautiful can come from a difficult journey. I love these little cakes as they are, but I'm all for adjusting recipes to make them your own so feel free to experiment with different flavours (for example, another filling other than ginger conserve) or to perhaps add buttercream on top. Enjoy!
    - Tori Haschka

Brown Sugar Swirl Cake with Buttercream Icing

Serves: 2
Prep Time: 40 mins
Cook Time: 40 mins

Food Groups:
sugars, fats,
carbohydrates

Instructions:

Heat oven to 175°C. Grease and flour 2 8-inch round cake pans.

Beat the flour, sugar, baking powder, salt, butter, milk, and vanilla in a stand mixer on low speed for 2 minutes. Add the eggs, and increase the speed to high for 2 more minutes, or until the mixture is smooth and lump free.

In a small bowl combine the brown sugar and melted butter. It should be pretty thick yet smooth. Fold into the cake mixture, trying to incorporate little bits throughout.

Pour into the prepared pans. Bake 30 to 40 minutes, or until golden on top and a cake tester comes out mostly clean. Remove the cakes from the oven and immediately run a sharp knife around the perimeter of the pans to loosen the cakes, then invert them on to a wire rack to cool completely.

While the cakes cool, make the frosting. Cream the butter until fluffy. Add the brown sugar and cinnamon; beat until it has become smooth in texture yet whipped.

Add three cups of the icing sugar, and mix on low speed so that you don't have a snowstorm. Stir in the vanilla extract, salt, and cream. Stir until incorporated.

Start by generously frosting the top of one of the cakes; layer the second on top of that, and then frost the whole thing all over.

Ingredients:

Cake

- 250g all purpose flour
- 250g granulated (white) sugar
- 3 1/2 teaspoons baking powder
- 1 1/2 teaspoons salt
- 125g butter, softened
- 250ml milk
- 1 teaspoon vanilla
- 4 eggs
- 2 tablespoons brown sugar
- 1 tablespoon melted butter

Icing

- 250g butter, at room temperature
- 125g light brown sugar, packed
- 1 teaspoon cinnamon
- 400-500g icing sugar
- 1 teaspoon vanilla extract
- 1/8 teaspoon salt
- 50ml whipping cream

When I was young, my mother made us very elaborate birthday cakes that featured multiple tiers, artful piping, buttercream roses. Because these intricate affairs would require days to make, she would reserve some of the mixture to make cupcakes, which were meant to tide the family over until the big cake was ready. Well, even at a young age, I had a complicated relationship with these cupcakes. Re-learning to trust myself around cake was a process that involved a bunch of therapy, a good support system, and oddly enough, teaching myself how to bake, which is the basis of my blog, CakeSpy.com. At first, I was too scared to try anything I made. But as I continued with my hobby, I began to fear cake and baked goods less. It became clear that it wasn't evil within cake, but normal things: sugar, butter, flour, eggs. I began getting brave, and taking tastes. I eat something sweet every day. Not because I need it, but because I want it, and because I've come to learn that sometimes we deserve things just because they're delicious and will give us pleasure. And when I look at it that way, a single slice isn't a sin. This is the cake I made for my birthday a few years back, and it remains a favourite.

- Jessie Moore

Queen of Puddings

This is a recipe my nan made that just used everyday ingredients from the larder, including bread that was no good for sandwiches. Amazing how delicious such simple ingredients can be.

- Thereza Baker

Serves: 4 - 6
Prep Time: 50 mins
Cook Time: 30 mins

Food Groups:
sugars, fruits

Ingredients:

- 200ml milk
- 200g breadcrumbs
- grated rind of 1 lemon
- 15g butter
- 15g sugar
- 2 egg yolks
- 2 tablespoon jam

For the meringue:

- 2 egg whites
- 55g castor sugar

Instructions:

Preheat the oven to 190°C and grease a pie dish with a knob of butter.

Heat the milk and pour it on to the breadcrumbs in the dish, add the lemon rind, butter and sugar and leave aside for about 30 minutes for the bread to swell.

Beat in the egg yolks and pour into the dish. Bake for 30 minutes until set.

Spread a layer of jam on the top, heating the jam if necessary, so that it will spread easily. Whisk the egg whites until very stiff, then fold 1 –2 tablespoon of the sugar.

Pile on top of the pudding and dredge with the remaining sugar.

Return to a the oven for 20 - 30 minutes until the meringue is lightly coloured and crisp to the touch.

FRUIT COCKTAILS

Fun and fruity with a big dollop of nostalgia for us big kids! Can easily be made before work and ready to eat when you get home, so there's no excuse not to have something you like!
- Jamie Malcolm

Serves: 4
Prep Time: 10 mins
Cook Time: 60 - 90 mins chill

Food Groups:
sugars, fruits

Ingredients:

- packet of jelly
- packet of Angel Delight
- 400g tin of fruit cocktail
- 250 ml hot water
- 250 ml cold water
- 300 ml milk

Toppings:

- sprinkles
- chocolate curls
- desiccated coconut
- whipped cream

Instructions:

Remove the fruit from the tin and separate equally between 4 mini bowls. Drink the remaining juice if you'd like!

Put the hot water into a measuring jug and add the cubes of jelly and stir until dissolved.

Add the cold water, mix again and pour evenly into the 4 dishes.

Set in the fridge for an hour or so or leave in there during the day.

Mix up the Angel Delight with 300ml of milk and pour evenly over the jelly.

Leave to set for 5 minutes and you can grate some chocolate or drop some sprinkles on top for some added nostalgia.

NITTY GRITTY

CONTRIBUTORS

All recipes, design, support, marketing and design have been donated for free, inr order to ensure that as much money can be raised to support B-EAT and their brilliant work. The following people have created this book.

—

Tina Klaus, (Don't Live Small www.dontlivesmall), Chris Sandel, (Seven Health www.seven -health.com), Bek Young, Katie Dalebout, (Wellness Wonderland www.thewellnesswonderland.com), Rebecca Pierson, Jodie Blight, (Hello Table www.hellotable.com.au), Christine Bailey, (Christine Bailey, www.christinebailey.co.uk), Tu Dinh Tran, (Eat the Globe, www.eattheglobe.com), Jennie Southwood, (Wholesome & Clean, www.wholesomeandclean.com.au), Michael Smith (www.chefmichaelsmith.com), Rosa Brown, John Linkins, Jimmy Eckersley, Miriam Roelink, (Recovery Warriors, www.recoverywarriors.com), Charlotte Maughan - Jones, Caroline Marson, Maxine, Ruby Tuesday, And Then She Disappeared, (www.andthenshedisappeared.blogspot.co.uk), Thereza Baker, Jamie Malcolm, Javier Orti, Laurel Alper, Tina Klaus, (Don't Live Small, www.dontlivesmall.com), Catherine Cowie, Jennifer Duke, (Jennifer Duke, www.twitter.com/jennieduke), Jessie Moore, (Cake Spy, www.cakespy.com/) Joseph Reddington, (www.joehreddington.com) Dana Bisenius, (Mantra Movement, www.mantramovement.com) Julia Norman, (Body Karma Healing, www.bodykarmahealing.com) Phoebe Labine, (Feed Me Phoebe, www.feedmephoebe.com), Sarah Wilson, (Slow Cooker Cookbook, www.sarahwilson.com), Shani Raviv, (Becoming Ana, www.shaniraviv.com), Tabitha Farrar, (www.tabithafarrar.com), Nina Mills, (What's For Eats, www.whatsforeats.com.au/) Michael Baker, Nikki Du Bose, (www.thenikkidebose.com), Tori Haschka, (Eatori, www.eatori.com), Peter Darling, Therese Higgins

—

Thank you. A thousand times thank you x

For more information about B-EAT, their work, and eating disorders, please
visit www.b-eat.co.uk
A helpline is available 0345 634 1414

f

To find out more about this project or any of by work, get in touch at
fbaker@live.co.uk
www.andsoshethinks.co.uk

Disclaimer

This book is provided for general information only. The information is not intended to be used as a substitute for professional medical advice, diagnosis, or treatment. Eating disorders are serious mental and physical illnesses that require medical and psychological support. If you are worried about yourself or anyone else, please seek help.

Made in the USA
San Bernardino, CA
04 April 2016